EROTIC LOVE POEMS *from* INDIA

A TRANSLATION OF THE
Amarushataka

ANDREW SCHELLING

SHAMBHALA
Boston & London
2004

FRONTISPIECE: *Radha-Krishna*, ca. 1735–1757, used by permission of the Philadelphia Museum of Art.

SHAMBHALA PUBLICATIONS, INC.
Horticultural Hall
300 Massachusetts Avenue
Boston, Massachusetts 02115
www.shambhala.com

© 2004 by Andrew Schelling

Poems 38,46,54,68,81,84,86,87, and 97 originally appeared in
The Cane Groves of Narmada River, © 1998 by Andrew Schelling.
Reprinted by permission of City Lights Books.

9 8 7 6 5 4 3 2 1

PRINTED IN SINGAPORE
First Edition
♾ This edition is printed on acid-free paper that meets
the American National Standards Institute z39.48 Standard.
Distributed in the United States by Random House, Inc.,
and in Canada by Random House of Canada Ltd

Library of Congress Cataloging-in-Publication Data
Amaru.
[Amaruṣataka. English]
Erotic love poems from India: a translation of the Amarushataka/
translated by Andrew Schelling
p. cm.
Includes bibliographical references.
In English; translated from Sanskrit.
ISBN 1-59030-097-1 (hardcover: alk. paper)
1. Sanskrit—Translations into English. I. Schelling, Andrew. II. Title.
PK3791.A43A812 2004
891'.21—dc22
2004006979

This book is for Marlow Brooks.
"If love be not in the house there is nothing."

nasty acauraḥ kavijanaḥ
There is no poet
who is not a thief.

—Rajashekhara

CONTENTS

INTRODUCTION

Love and the Turning Seasons

"IT IS WELL KNOWN," writes the ninth-century Kashmiri yogin and literary critic Anandavardhana, "that a single stanza of the poet Amaru . . . may provide the taste of love equal to what's found in whole volumes." This statement, from his seminal work on Sanskrit poetics, the *Dhvanyaloka*, is the first historic mention of the author to whom the verses in this volume are commonly attributed. The collection, known in Sanskrit as the *Amarushataka* ("One Hundred Poems of Amaru"), was compiled in the eighth century and remains to this day one of the celebrated books of poetry in India. It has never before been translated in its entirety into English verse.

The popular account of the anthology's origin is so vivid, precise, and magical it could only have come from South Asia. It is said that the venerable Shankara (788–820), India's formidable master of Advaita Vedanta, or Nondual Philosophy, was locked in public debate with Mandanamishra, an advocate of a rival school of philosophy, the Mimamsa. Shankara was roundly defeating his opponent when Mandanamishra's wife entered the fray. A sly and sportive lady, she posed a series of metaphysical questions to Shankara, couched in detailed metaphors of sexual love. Shan-kara, being celibate, was silenced. He applied for an adjournment of a hundred days and nights to prepare a suitable response.

Leaving the stage and entrusting his body to his disciples, Shankara employed his yogic powers to enter the corpse of a just-deceased Kashmiri king named Amaru, already lying on an unlit funeral pyre. Amaru's body quickened—thrilling the harem girls of Srinagar and Jammu, no doubt—and Shankara in the borrowed form spent a hundred nights studying love at first hand, each with a different lady of Amaru's court. He devoted his daytime hours to a careful examination of Vatsyayana's *Kama Sutra* and its commentaries. When his hundred nights had come to an end, Shankara added a few additional ones—for good luck, or simply to further his studies. Then he abandoned Amaru's body to its fate and returned to his own.

Taking the stage of debate again, Shankara proved himself adept at the science that had once eluded him, and vanquished his opponents. It is said that he composed a poem to memorialize the lesson of each of those nights. Once he had gathered his poems into a volume, he signed the collection with Amaru's name—a touch of gratitude for the lessons received at Amaru's court, through the king's awakened senses.

This story first appears in a fourteenth-century hagiography of Shankara, the *Shankara-digvijaya* by Madhava (also known as Vidyaranya). A somewhat later commentator on the *Amarushataka*, Ravichandra, provides an alternative account. In his version Shankara pays a visit to the court of the Kashmiri king. Amaru, a great sensualist as well as a warlord, was known to devote his waking hours to his carefully selected court ladies. Hoping to improve his epicurean host's spiritual insight, Shankara devises a hundred instructive poems in which he articulates metaphysical teachings in the conventional language of love—a lesson proposed in terms Amaru might understand. After Shankara recites the verses, the king's advisers and courtiers, too dull to catch the subtle intent, mock Shankara for composing a cycle of love poetry. If the renowned celibate has held to his vows, how could he detail such intimacies? Shankara fills with rage at their small-mindedness. Through his yogic powers he seizes Amaru's body and delivers a spiritual exegesis of his poems through the king's mouth. And Amaru, hearing his own throat give angry vent to such teachings, is transformed on the spot.

The best research by contemporary scholarship dates the *Amarushataka* to about the year 750 CE. Indian scholars since Anandavardhana's time have attributed the work to a single poet, his name given as Amaru, Amaruka, or Amaraka. Tradition reads it as a single poem, or more properly, a cycle of interlocked stanzas that lead the reader along a carefully charted course. All the flavors or nuances of love are said to lie within the book, though you'll notice that the emphasis falls more on the bitter taste of separation or betrayal than on the sweetness of consummation.

A survey of what has been written discloses that the provenance of South Asian manuscripts is a complicated affair. Scholars remain divided on the most elemental details: when the Amaru collection was put together, by whom, and where. Most Western scholars regard it as an anthology, considering Amaru a compiler who may have included some of his own poems. Indian scholars continue to credit a single author and to read it as a unified cycle.

Whatever its origins, for thirteen hundred years this work has retained its reputation in India as one of the foundational collections of poetry. It is indispensable for any literate person with a classical education. Poets and critics still use its verses as a template against which to consider other poems. For our own era, it shows that long years ago India developed a love poetry original and vivid as that produced anywhere on the planet.

Only partly evident upon a first reading of the *Amarushataka* is a hint of what holds together not only these verses of love and longing, but all of India's old poetry: the presence of the revolving year.

Love and the turning seasons. This theme might serve, in more ways than one, as a gateway through which to approach the *Amarushataka*. Its poems do indeed portray the revolution of a calendar cycle, as do so many Asian anthologies. Yet it is the cyclic migrations of the human heart that receive the most considered treatment. Monsoon rainstorms and the winds that announce them, the aromatic unfolding of jasmine creepers or a dozen species of water lotus, the mating songs of peacock and kingfisher—these rise and subside in the poems of old India like the chant of an archaic chorus. The central drama remains human.

In India the love god is named Kama, Desire. He has many epithets, one of them Ananga, Bodiless, because he slips unseen through the world with the hunter's bow and arrows. His consort is Rati, Sexual Pleasure. At Kama's appearance, growling, tenebrous storm clouds mount the horizon, signaling the onset of monsoon season. The heat-withered vegetation rewakens, aromatic flowers unfurl their petals, wild animals go into rut, and lightning creases the boiling dark sky. Driven by cool winds, intoxicating fragrances plunge down from forested mountain ranges, and pollinating insects thread the meadows and riparian groves.

And humans? Humans in our sexual rapture—even our anguish—recuperate the oldest and most durable of traditions. This tradition, a ceremonial dance of fertility, antedates any known religion. Pursuing love we enact a camaraderie with the planet's sentient creatures. Even the geologic upheavals that produce mountain ranges, or the little-understood ocean currents that drive the weather through its yearly cycle, are stirred by the force that stirs the cicada, the antelope, the gods, and us.

This is why the poets of classical India regarded love as the first and deepest of passions, and the foremost theme for poetry. Love keeps humans, with our large well-organized brains and rich speculative ability, grounded in the biological world. It prevents us from slipping too far into mental abstraction. Kama, whose bow is the demonstrative eyebrow of a woman or the curved tines of the antelope, whose arrows come tipped with blossoming lotuses, whose agents are aroma-charged winds and charcoal-colored thunderheads, is the manifestation of procreative, generative Nature.

Kama must be an old Indo-European figure. He surfaces as Eros in Greece, Amor to the Romans. With a quick slip of gender he becomes Diana, Goddess of the Hunt, also depicted as a wielder of the bow.

The hunter's recursive bow, and variations of the self-bow and longbow, have been known to both Eastern and Western Hemispheres since the last Ice Age. For thousands of years in southern Europe it has been shown in the hands of the goddess

Venus, and is both instrument and symbol of the two arts of venery: love and the hunt. Linger over the Indo-European origins of the word a moment, and notice the vocabulary it gives rise to. *Venus* is the planet that governs erotic love. *Venison* is the wild animal in rut. *Venom* was originally a love potion. In India, *vanam* means sexual delight and remains the common word for forest. *Venery, venereal.* Observe the close association of the chase and the hunt with fertility. Humans have looked to the realm of magic to ensure success in love and in the taking of large game—those two intertwined mysteries— since at least the Upper Paleolithic, when, according to archaeological evidence, the earliest surviving bows were crafted.

Bow fragments dated at eleven thousand years before the present have been unearthed in peat bogs of Northern Europe. The oldest come from Denmark, Germany, and the British Isles, where the anaerobic environment of the bogs preserved the highly degradable materials: wood, resin, and sinew. The bow itself could conceivably be a much older weapon, but archaeological evidence simply wouldn't have survived. Given its centrality for survival in cultures that knew the bow—and its astonishing ability to take down prey at a distance—a rich collection of magical lore has accumulated around its use. It is difficult to say, at this remove from its first appearance, when a deity armed with bow and arrows emerged on the Eurasian continent. But he or she must be an archaic figure indeed.

How curious that the deity of the bow got pressed to the margins of religious ceremony long ago by official religion and its curators, both East and West. Stranger still that with no church, no priesthood, no altar, no ritual, the god of venery remains vivid to poetic and popular imagination. Look for him as the consort of Psyche in the Greek mystery stories; look for him in Chaucer's tales, in Shakespeare's; look for him in Kalidasa's *Kumara-sambhava* ("Birth of the War God") where the story is told of how the love god became bodiless. See his image everywhere on St. Valentine's Day. In the *Amarushataka*, the goddess Mridani and the ferociously outfitted god Shiva conspicuously appear in the opening verses as wielders of the bow and arrow. In this guise they get called upon first to protect lovers (or is it readers of poetry?), then to burn off their infelicities.

Could all the cold, far-seeing deities of Mount Kailash and all the quarrelsome gods of Mount Olympus be in the end no more than servants of Kama? As though five thousand years of organized religion were only a detour? How fitting that the *Amarushataka*'s two closing stanzas belong to him— the tracker and hunter—the "holy god of love."

The world of India's art is a topsy-turvy place. It comfortably holds contradictions that pale moralizing or humorless logic find intolerable most everywhere else. Religious texts use erotic language with blazing specificity; erotic poems come couched in precise theological terms. Sandstone and chlorite sculptures of teeming figures—human and animal, in pairs or in groups—enjoying explicit physical love, mount the towers of holiest temples at Khajuraho, Konarak, and elsewhere. With complex, coded language spiritual adepts protect the most advanced erotic practices. So who is to say that profound spiritual insights may not be woven into the heartbreak and humor of the *Amarushataka*?

Or might humor and heartbreak be enough? Amaru, the elusive eighth-century poet, is said to have been a warlord in the strategic valley of Kashmir, with Pathan warriors to the west, Rajput warriors to the south, and tough mountain tribes north and east. He ruled a notable dynasty in his day; he may have fought hand-to-hand in combat; and with cold military precision he could have sent obedient soldiers to their deaths. The centuries have swallowed what military or political success this ruler achieved. Yet the volume of poetry he sculpted survives—as though delivered into the twenty-first century by the ghost-hands of a warrior.

I wonder. When we who are currently living have passed through this world—through an era that seems unprecedented for its wars, its political corruption, its injustice, its senseless mishandling of plant and animal species—I wonder if what remains most vivid at the end won't be a few moments of utterly vulnerable humor and tender heartbreak. Two or three stanzas of poetry.

ANDREW SCHELLING
Boulder, Colorado
May Day, 2004

ACKNOWLEDGMENTS

I WANT TO THANK both the publishers and the readers of journals where a number of these poems first appeared: *a.bacus*, *Bombay Gin*, *Circumference*, and *Shiny*, as well as the online periodical *CipherJournal*. Deep gratitude goes to the Witter Bynner Foundation for Poetry for providing a grant in 2001 to help with this project. Thanks to Naropa University for a seed grant used to pursue research in the Oriental and India Office of the British Library. I owe a further debt of gratitude to Kristen Anderson and Kika Silva, students at the Jack Kerouac School, for providing clearheaded suggestions and wily encouragement on the manuscript as it developed. Three bows of the head to my patient editors at Shambhala, Liz Shaw and Peter Turner, who capably helped turn the manuscript into a book.

Erotic Love
Poems from India

I

THE goddess Mridani
takes the archer's *katakamukha* pose—
bending the bowstring
back to her ear.
Red nails
by her ear a cluster of moist
glistening petals.
And her greedy blue side-darting
eye like a hornet—
May it protect you.

NOTE: Mridani, the wife of Shiva, is one name for the
Goddess, whose many other manifestations include Parvati,
Durga, or Kali. In some guises Shiva's consort appears as a
fearsome warrior as well as a voluptuous lover.

   The *katakamukha* pose, known to classical dance and to
yoga, is simply "(bow) string to the mouth."

   This verse serves as the first of four invocations in the
Amarushataka to one or another of the gods.

2

SHAKEN off it clung
to their hands,
batted away it clutched
the hems of their robes,
rejected it caught at their hair.
When it fell at their feet they refused
in agitation to look.
Though dismissed it wrapped around the
teary blue-lotus-eyed girls
of Tripura citadel.
Not a lover caught
cheating but the fire of Shiva's arrows—
May it burn off your
            indiscretions.

NOTE: Central to the mythology of Shiva is his destruction
of the stronghold of demons, Tripura, or the Three Cities,
one built of gold, one silver, one iron, all magically linked to-
gether. Shiva caused a vast conflagration in the triple citadel
by releasing a single flaming arrow empowered with mantras
into its midst.

3

FRONT curls tossed in disorder
earrings scattered
beads of sweat smearing the sandal
paste on her brow—
now her eyes droop as astride her
companion she finishes.
May the face of this lady protect you.
Vishnu, Shiva, Brahma,
the gods
mean nothing.

4

TENDER lip bitten she
shakes her fingers alarmed—
hisses a fierce
don't you dare and her
eyebrows leap like a vine.
Who steals a kiss from a
proud woman flashing her eyes
drinks *amrita*.
The gods—fools—
churned the ocean for
nothing.

NOTE: After enormous labor, the gods collectively managed
to raise *amrita*, the drink of immortality (Greek: *ambrosia*),
from the ocean floor. They secured it in the moon, away from
the grasp of their enemies, the *asuras*, who would appropriate
it. As a life-bestowing fluid on the moon, *amrita* became
identified with *soma*, the potent vision-inducing drink of the
Vedas. Precious, generative fluids, both *amrita* and *soma* hold
strong sexual implications—the juices of life.

5

TREMBLING with awakened love
they dart off,
then contract into two moist buds.
An instant they shamelessly stare,
a moment glisten with shy indirection.
Dear girl so artless—
who is it you look at
as though the feverish spell lodged
in your heart
had rushed to your eyes?

6

W HY weep in silence
striking aside
angry tears with your fingernails?
When spurred by cheap gossip this fit
gets completely out of hand,
your lover will
tire and grow grim and indifferent.
Then your tears will break
violently,
out of control.

7

You provided love,
you touched her
intimately for a long time.
Now in a fatal twist
you've inflicted the most savage wound.
Tender words can't assuage
her unbearable jealousy.
Our friend needs to cry now—
grief has
unlocked her throat.

8

YOUR lover sits
dejected
scratching figures in the dirt outside.
Your friends won't eat
their eyes are swollen from crying.
There's no silly chatter from the
household parrots
and you're a wreck.
Stubborn girl, isn't it
time to quit
sulking?

9

Women of intrepid
charm
can't be stopped—
they'll even steal what they want.
Why be timid? Tears cannot bring
satisfaction.
You want him,
he's hungry for sexual pleasure—
try some crudely explicit suggestion
and make
him your own.

10

She binds him
in her arms
pliant as tendrils.
It happened again.
Stammering in front of her friends
she draws him into the bedroom,
his misconduct apparent.
Lucky man—
the crying girl hits him
he laughs and denies
          everything.

11

Don't those who depart
always return?
Sweet creature, you fret and are
wasting away. . . .
I stammered through tears.
She stared blankly
swallowing her own emotion.
Shame lay across her dark pupils.
Then a dry desperate laugh
said it all—
she intended to die.

12

Forcing my face
from his
I glared at his feet.
Desperate for his voice I closed
my ears, even hid the
sweat on my cheeks with my palms.
But friends, what could I do—?
Where my thin top
gathers my breasts a hundred
stitches had split.

13

AFTER *the first watch,*
the middle,
or is it toward dusk you return?
Not gone the whole day?
Words choked with emotion she
stalls his departure.
And he's intent
on a district
a hundred days off.

14

W$_E$ were making love
when something hurt. I cried
get away!
He tore himself
from the bed and departed.
Impetuous, pitiless, he tramples on romance—
but my heart
craves him shamelessly,
what do I do?

15

ALL night the two of them
exchanged
intimate words—
now dawn
the household parrot
chatters it out to the in-laws.
She slips a ruby
from her ear, horrified,
into the parrot's beak—
it could be a pomegranate seed—
and stifles the
unconstrained cries.

16

STUPIDLY, out of
sheer wickedness—
my face turned in grief—
you embrace me.
What does cheating get?
It comes down to this—
your chest
streaked with tawny
paste from your girlfriend's breasts
now smudged with
oil from my braid ends.

17

Rising to greet him—
still far off—
she avoided sharing a couch.
When he reached for her
off she ran for betel nut leaf.
Nor could he speak to her
so diligent was she
to the servants' instructions.
Shrewd girl, every courtesy
applied just
to get back at him.

18

RASCAL,
he slips behind his two
seated lovers.
A playful advance—
he covers the eyes of one—
then turning his neck
kisses the other.
A deep erotic thrill goes through
her cheeks
the flush of a
secret smile.

19

W<small>HEN</small> she'd been icy he
dropped at her feet.
But accused of cheating in secret
he bristled and
left. She exhaled audibly
both hands on her breasts
and glanced
through moist eyes at
her girlfriends.

20

WHY is this enchanted
creature asleep,
a sash fastened over her robe?
He was softly querying
the servants
when she cried bitterly
Mother, he disrupts my dreams even here!
and turned as if
sleeping to make room
on the bed.

21

Each turned aside
on the bed
silently suffering
secretly hoping to reconcile but
afraid to lose face.
At some point their furtive eyes met—
there was a quick
unintentional laugh and the
quarrel broke
in one wild embrace.

22

Thinking I'd see how
she took it
I put on a hard implacable look.
Why can't this snake even talk to me—?
said the glare on her face.
Charming stand-off
eyeing each other warily.
When I gave an impious
grin she lost her nerve and broke
into tears.

23

IN bed he whispers
the wrong name.
She feels her youthful enthusiasm wilt
and curls coldly away
from excuses.
He falls silent.
And she turning back softly
eyes him—
Don't go to sleep.

24

W<small>HY</small> fall at my feet?
You can't hide
the unguent from her nipples
streaking your chest.
Where? I said rising quickly—
and to rub it away
took her fiercely. Rough
pleasure—
the slender creature
forgot everything.

25

YOUR eyes enchant me.
Remove this camisole and
take my glamorized heart
captive.
He fingered her
knotted braid as he spoke.
Delighted by radiant
eyes and quick smile of their friend—
perched at the end of her bed—
the other ladies with soft
excuses
withdrew.

26

Scowling I knot up
my forehead
but this traitorous eye shamelessly lifts.
I refuse words but
my rebellious face softens.
Make a stone of my heart
and on its own
this aroused body tingles.
Anger just
can't keep its grip
when that boy
comes into view.

27

THE lord of her heart
made some
injurious remark.
Lacking the counsel of friends
she could not compose her bewildered
body or phrase
a slant reply.
Blue eye petals darting about
she just wept—
tears on bright cheekbones
locks of stray hair.

28

Now I know everything.
Please go. Talking is pointless.
You don't bear the
slightest blame,
fate has simply turned from me.
Since your so abundant love
comes to this
what pain could I experience
if hateful life—
mere flicker of nature—
                were to depart?

29

Milky chatter
of pearls
at your breasts
over your belly a jangling belt
gemstones clattering along your trim ankles.
If you set off with a drum roll
to meet your lover
why do you tremble, child—
as though every
slight shadow
might catch you?

30

Dawn after dawn
our lovemaking
took the sleep from my eyes.
A weight lifted.
For once my heart felt light.
Now what have you done?
Go—you are foolish and miserable
and death no longer scares me.
One day you may hear
down which road
I've decided to go.

3 1

M<small>Y</small> bracelets are gone.
Tears, those sweet friends, departed forever.
Courage left instantly
and my heart
went fastest of all.
They set off in concert
when my beloved decided
to leave.
You should go too, life—
why lag behind that troop
of dear comrades?

32

*H*E sleeps, dear,
    you should sleep too.
My girlfriends withdrew and
a wild hunger
consumed me. I pressed
my mouth to his.
But he was already aroused—
I felt it—he'd shut his eyes
to deceive us!
How shy I got—
but he dispelled it with touches
the late
hour warranted.

33

THOSE days a slanted brow
meant anger,
silence a quarrel,
two smiles forgiveness.
Grace was held in
a glance.

Look at the wreckage
that's come of love.
You at my feet groveling,
me thrashing about
in frustrated anger.

34

Sweetheart, please speak.
Look at me
collapsed at your feet.
Your anger never gets this bad—
He was pleading.
She winced, jerked her tearful
eyes aside
and said nothing.

35

Her breasts
flattened against me
her flesh seemed to ripple,
at her thighs the sheer
silk parted.
I heard a mute *don't—*
don't—this is enough for me—
      did she sleep, did she die then?
sink into my heart?
completely dissolve?

36

SHE averts a well-bred face
when her lord
fingers her skirt.
He moves to enfold her,
she extracts
her limbs mildly.
Caught wordless,
eyeing the conspiratorial smiles
of her bridesmaids,
at a first joke the girl
      nearly perishes.

37

No kindness no word
of endearment
could soothe her bruised pride.
All day long
her heart strangled.
Two faces averted but
who can say how
the sidelong glance meets?
A smile
a quick laugh
and indignation was
banished.

38

Love's bond is broken.
The heart's high
passion has waned.
Even truth is a ghost
when that man
walks past like someone unknown.
Days long vanished rise up
dear friend to haunt me
and why this heart
doesn't splinter into a hundred shards
who can tell?

39

T HE young lovers,
bodies a long time aching apart,
are now reunited.
How utterly
new the world seems and the
long day drifts past unnoticed.
            At nightfall
they put off
for later their stories,
not so their lovemaking.

40

WITH dark eyes
not blue lotus
she fashions a welcome garland.
Petals she strews—
not various species of jasmine
but smiles.
Water she offers from ripe
sweating breasts
rather than ceremonial jars.
With only her own body
she makes for her
lover a
propitious arrival.

41

AT twilight today
he deceived me.
I'd banished him for some offense
and he returned in my
girlfriend's clothes.
Naive, clasping the imposter,
I confided how urgently I wanted
to sleep with him.
"That will be hard to achieve—"
A laugh in the
darkness
he forcibly took me.

42

Suspecting I might
fall at her feet
she deftly folds them beneath her skirt
hides a sly smile
won't glance upward.
To avoid answering she chats
with a girlfriend. If
displeased she's this luscious—
imagine
her passionate.

43

INSTRUCTED by servants—
skilled liars—
she chatters a quick excuse to her
difficult husband.
Then to perform what the love god requests. . . .
This is love's
inmost enchantment—
innocence
adorns it.

44

WHEN a lover is faithless
the eye in an
instant changes its theme.
He's far off, it's restless,
he arrives,
it turns to the side,
dilates if he speaks,
reddens when he attempts
an embrace.
He clutches her robe and its brow
twists like a vine.
He falls to the angry
woman's feet
      it wells up with tears.

45

Your *body so thin*
trembling
and cheeks pale as ash—?
When the lord of her life confronts her
the slim girl says *these*
things just happen
turns and between her eyelashes
catches the tears
for someplace else.

46

Night
turbulent overhead clouds
and a ripple of thunder.
The traveler
stung with tears
sings of a faraway girl.
Oh traveling
is a kind of death,
the village people hear it,
lower their heads
         and quit talking.

47

WE'D been drinking.
She noticed wounds on my skin
from her own
fingernails
and bolted up jealously.
Let go, she cried when I caught her skirt.
Tear-streaked face averted
lower lip quavering—
who could forget
      what she said next?

48

O TROUBLED heart!
At the door of the hut
full of hungry affection he dropped
at these feet.
And you denied him?
Now anger and vanity come into fruit.
Now love is a vagabond.
Grief will be your solitary
refuge
through life.

49

THROUGH tears
she saw mist
and the clustering
rainclouds. *If you leave . . .*
her voice trailed and she clung
to my jacket,
scuffing the parched earth
where she dug in.
What she did next
no poet's words command
the power to tell.

50

D<small>EAR</small> girl—
My lord?
Stop being bitter and proud.
What does my bitterness do?
Troubles me.
You don't mistreat me the
*   faults are mine.*
Why tears and whimpering then?
Can anyone see me?
I can.
And am to you—?
My dearest.
That's why the tears.
*   I am not.*

51

*T*HAT *precious throat I was too*
shy to caress—
when he kissed
why did I drop my face,
not look up, not even speak?
Thoughts of her childish demeanor
as a bride are weighed
with regret.
Her heart has flowered now.
She's tasted the sweet
      arts of the bedroom.

52

UNHAPPY women
have used tears, threatening oaths,
even collapse
to prevent a lover
from traveling.
Darling, I'm a pluckier girl.
Good luck and for your
early departure
I hope an auspicious day.
After you're gone you may hear
what I see fit to do with my
love life.

53

SHE did not clutch
his soft robe in a tendril-like hand,
block the door,
fall at his feet bitterly,
or cry *stay!*
As slow tenebrous clouds built in the
sky and her deceitful lover
was starting out
she cut off his path with
a violent
torrent of tears.

54

THE love god has made
everything crooked.
Apart from you I get thinner and thinner.
It must be Yama the death god who
counts out our days.
How does a woman
survive without trust?
I tremble, darling,
　　　　　a single green leaf on a twig.

NOTE: In Indian folklore, Yama serves as lord of the under-world. See the opening passage of the *Katha Upanishad* for one of his early appearances.

55

ANGER subsided.
She held a moonlit face in both hands.
I'd collapsed to the
earth in despair.
Suddenly across her breasts teardrops
broke from
thick lashes.
We were at peace.

56

I WAS still at a distance
and you rose
smiling
to greet with calm words
my requests.
In bed your eyes never softened though.
Your anger scorches me.
In that heart coils
something deceptive.

57

FRIENDS I no longer trust.
I'm too shy
to toss a playful glance
at the one who fires
my passion.
People are quick to mock—
the slightest
indiscretion gets noted.
Oh mother, where can I hide?
The flames
of desire ungratified
wither the heart.

58

HEAR his name
and every hair on my
body's aroused.
See his moonlike face
I get moist like a moonstone everywhere.
He steps near enough to touch
my throat
and pride is broken oh hard
diamond heart.

NOTE: In Indian folklore the moonstone is said to secrete
moisture when struck by a moonbeam.

59

SURELY in all these houses
girls are coming
of age.
Go inquire: do their
lovers submit to them
the way this slave does?
You've let the wicked
speak into your ear and disfigure you—
any more trouble a man
might lose
his taste for love.

60

Love is a swollen
river—
urgent, nearly touching
the lovers stand thwarted.
Parents like embankments
hold them back.
Face to face
motionless as paintings
they drink love's
nectar through lotus-stalk eyes.

61

THE sandal paste
is rubbed from your lifted
breasts,
your lip rouge is smeared,
the kohl's gone from your eyes.
Deceitful messenger
your soft skin's aroused
and you can't see your own
sister's despair!
Tell me you went to the
bathing tank
not back
to that scoundrel.

62

HER cheerless pinched face,
lifeless hair
falling like cinders about it,
brightened the moment I returned
from abroad.
That slender girl's mouth—
who could forget the sweet moisture,
we drank
love so eagerly.

63

Tнough chafing
she no longer struggles if I
loosen her skirt.
No scowling no
biting the lip when her
hair's gripped.
Even opens her
limbs compliantly and doesn't
resist when I'm rough.
What is this
new expression of anger?

64

Thoughts and
emotions disordered
she wordlessly rebukes the lover
who's lowered himself
at her feet.
When he rises to go
she's quite limp
eyes clouded with relentless tears—
thin and unsteady
she stands in his way.

65

Scarlet betel-nut juice
spattered about,
black streaks of sandalwood oil,
smears of camphor,
and imprints
from the henna designs on her feet.
In scattered folds petals
lost from her hair.
Every position a
woman took pleasure from
is told on
these bed sheets.

66

TELL you a secret—
he called me to a secluded seat.
My childlike curious heart fluttered
drawing near.
He spoke in my ear
breathed near my mouth
then, friend, he seized these braids
and sucked the
honey off my lips.

67

FEELING the quick
flush of her period she stood
off from the bed.
His eyebrows begged
an intimate kiss,
his lip trembled.
Shaking her head no—
clutching a shawl to bright cheeks
the many glittering pendants
at her ears.

68

Where to
girl with bright thighs?
There's no moon tonight.

Out to my lover.

Not afraid, young in the darkness
to travel alone?

Can't you see—at my side
with lethal arrows the
love god?

69

Tᴉʟᴛᴇᴅ his head
when she cast a vine-knotted
brow at her rival.
Saluted and stood
abstractly off
when somebody noticed.
Her cheeks flashed like copper.
He stared at her feet.
Yet in front of the parents they
managed to keep up
appearances.

70

LONG minutes her
haunted eyes stared,
with clasped palms she pleaded,
clutched the white robe's
edge and held him tormentedly.
When he pushed her aside
and coldly started out
she let go first her hold
on life
then him.

71

SHE sees smudges of lac on his brow,
on his neck
a bracelet's imprint,
on his cheek eyeblack
and scarlet streaks of betel-nut juice.
All morning long
she toys with a red lotus,
breathing
deep into its calyx.

72

FROM this day on
I'll be no refuge for
bitterness. I won't even shape
that man's poisonous
name in my mouth.
Lady Night sheds
bright laughing moon rays without him.
Can't I get through one
monsoon day darkened
with thunder?

73

WICKEDLY you drop
your arms from my waist
at the sound of somebody's
girdle gems.
And I can confide in no one.
My girlfriend's in a whirl.
She says it's nothing.
Your venomous words all butter and
honey have
softened her.

74

Finally their quarters
are empty.
She raises herself on the couch
studies his face at length
then searches his sleeping frame
with her mouth.
He isn't asleep though—
across one cheek
runs a quiver.
With a laugh he
kisses his
bride's downturned face.

75

Wʜʏ treat your man
with contempt
when he lies at your feet?
You think he's too
slow at love?
At her handmaid's rebuke
anger subsided. Tears pressed forward.
Suddenly she couldn't
restrain them
couldn't let go.

76

His replies sounded forced
when he got back.
In his absence she'd
grown lean
and contrived not to notice.
But fearful his evasions
might reach the ears
of judgmental friends, she
cast her eyes quickly about.
Nobody there.
She breathed again
deeply.

77

Look, delicate one, the bed is stained—
intimate love
has caked it with sandalwood powder.
Pulling me onto his chest
he bit my lip roguishly
tore off my gown with his feet
and again
started our raptures.

78

To the family her
endless tears,
to parents her bitterness,
affliction she's left
to the servants,
stabs of anguish to friends.
Tomorrow she may provide ecstasies
today it is sighs—
but be sure—
she's already handed around
all the suffering.

79

Lᴇᴛ this heart split,
friend—
let Kama twist my thin
body however he likes—
I'm done! Done with that man's
unreliable
comings and goings.

A burst of embittered words—
then in abrupt alarm
she searches with antelope eyes
the hidden
forest path.

Nᴏᴛᴇ: Kama (Desire) is the god of love, known by other ep-
ithets as well, such as Ananga (Bodiless) and Madana (Intox-
icator).

80

His lip
recklessly bruised by some
other girl's tooth?
She swings a yellow lotus angrily.
He stands
squeezing his eyes.
Did a filament get in—?
Remorse or is it
         shrewdness?
She blows softly at his face
through pursed lips.
And no he doesn't fall at
her feet he just
         kisses her.

81

THOSE first days
of untempered love
my body and
your body were never apart.
The seasons turned.
You came to be my cherished lord,
I the desolate mistress.
Now you're the husband,
I'm the wife, and the year
turns again?
Life must be cruel as a thunderbolt
if this is
where it ends.

82

You're determined
to lead your whole life
like a child?
Develop some pride,
take a risk.
With a lover you need to be devious.
Her face whitened
at her friend's admonishment.
Speak softly he'll hear you—
he dwells
in my heart.

83

By the courtyard well
she hangs onto a
spray from the mango tree.
Black female bees
greedy for loose pollen are swarming,
and I think the lady has wrapped
her slight body with a
bit of cloth.
Her breasts tremble—
she's choking back the sobs
in her throat.

84

You ignored
the turning seasons of love,
shook off counsel,
and treated your
lovers with cold disregard.
The coals of betrayal flare in your
own bare hands.
The planet is burning.
And now this intractable rage—
like a wild
wounded animal's.

85

You've rubbed
the feathery patterns from your
cheeks with your
own palms.
Sighs have removed the dew
that rises from within
to your parted lips.
Your breasts quaver but
it's from hard
tears in your throat.
Bitter girl, anger makes love
to you not I.

86

SOMEHOW she
got through the day
anticipating
the hundred pleasures of night.
Her dear one's returned!
But now it's time to enter the bedchamber
and relatives
won't stop their dull conversation.
Mad with desire the girl finally cries
something bit me
shakes her skirt fiercely
and knocks over
     the lamp—

87

My breasts at first
little buds
grew plump under your hands.
My speech
instructed by yours
lost its native simplicity.
What shall I do?
These arms
left my old nursemaid's neck
to creep around yours,
but you no longer
       set foot in the neighborhood.

88

WHEN my heart leaps at
a sight of her
and I devise a thousand ways to claim her—
when desire flares and the
messenger girl
brings explicit descriptions—
who could imagine the ecstasies
of a single quick night?
I walk the oxcart path
outside her house and obtain the
fiercest pleasure.

89

CAMISOLE shed to the floor,
she shakes—shakes—
a leaf-soft hand and casts her crushed
string of jasmine at the
lamp flame.
Disheveled but smiling
she covers his eyes.
Now that they've made love, again
and again his enraptured
eyes find her.

FACE turned aside
eyes squeezed angrily shut
she pretends she's asleep.
Into her thin legs and arms
with a clever motion he
inserts his own.
And when a trembling
hand goes to her waistband she
sucks her already
tight stomach tighter.

91

FAR as the eye can reach
she gazes down
the footpath her lover takes.
The roads have gone silent.
Day's given way to stealthy night.
She takes one reluctant step
homewards—
delayed a few minutes maybe—
snaps her head
around searching darkly.

92

KINGDOMS lie between them.
Hundreds of rivers, soaring peaks,
forests. Nothing
he tries could bring her
to view.
Why stand on tiptoe
on the good earth craning his neck?
The traveler rubs grit
from his eyes, he studies
the far horizon—
thinking—

93

S<small>WEAT</small> on your face?
>   *—the piercing sunshine.*
Your eyes look red and excited—
>   *—his tone made me furious.*
Your black hair scattered—
>   *—the wind.*
What about the saffron designs on your breasts?
>   *My blouse rubbed them off.*
And so winded—
>   *—from running back and forth.*
Of course.
But what's this curious
wound to your lip?

NOTE: A poem nearly identical in content though with quite different vocabulary, attributed to Lady Shilabhattarika (ca. ninth century), appears in several later anthologies. The theme of a jealous young woman and the messenger girl who has possibly betrayed her occurs often in Sanskrit poetry.

94

Hard-hearted girl
drop these suspicions, the stories
are false—
treacherous accounts
designed to bring discord.
If you're that impressionable
do as you like with me.
May it
bring peace.

95

KNOTTED my brows a long time,
learned to squint,
trained myself sedulously
to suppress smiles
even achieved the yoga
        of silence.
In my heart courage is fixed.
The stage is set, the attendants of anger
are gathered—
success now
lies with the gods.

96

HE'D drop at my feet,
cry and make oaths,
sweeten me with crazy words.
There'd be savage love for this
starved body and hard
kisses everywhere.
Angry displays bring compelling rewards
but dare I risk it—
this lover lies near my heart—
          can I toy with him?

97

My lover
stepped towards the bed.
Somehow the skirt
clung to my hips
but the knot came undone by itself.
What can I say?
Nothing makes sense in his arms
not who I am
not who is taking me.
Is it me that comes?
Is it him?

98

Sɪɢʜs parch my lips.
My uprooted
heart is torn out.
Sleep doesn't come, my lover's face
won't appear.
Night and day this husk of a
body weeps since he lay at my feet
rejected.
What were you thinking, friends—
goading me to
treat him so harshly?

99

S HE did nothing to
bar the door
did not turn her face away
there were no brittle words.
She just gazed with indifferent eyes through
steady lashes.
He could have been anyone.

100

WHEN he's frisky
and steals her undergarments
she squeals in distress
quick—before someone suspects!

But the love god sees,
        mighty archer of the three worlds,

and though the fortifications
are breached,
the erotic struggle decided,
he flashes back to the
        battlefield.

NOTE: In Indian mythology the three worlds, or *lokas,* are traditionally heaven, earth, and the underworld. One can't help appreciating the distinctness—and perhaps uniqueness—of a cosmology in which the love god goes armed with arrows, not through heaven and earth only, but even into the underworld.

101

Half mad with desire a young
woman raises her
leaf-soft foot—
anklet and cochineal tattoos—
and kicks him for some offense.
Thus is a man claimed
by the god with the crocodile banner,
the holy
god of love.

NOTE: Crocodile? Some give it as dolphin or sea monster. The Sanskrit word is *makara*, a "hybrid aquatic creature" of mythology. Like a crocodile but unlike the dolphin, the *makara* has teeth.

AFTERWORD

TO EXAMINE ONE OF THE POEMS attributed to
Amaru is to glimpse a single charged instant in the
human drama. A lifetime can seem compressed into
those few measured words. From them, threads of
passion wind deep into the past, or maddeningly into
the future. It is not just the psychological precision
found in such a small poem. It's the skill in devising
a minute artifact that yet feels as though it contains
the dimensions of a human life.

I want to speak about the origins of the *Ama-
rushataka* poems. My first thought is that upon en-
tering their world, one instantly recognizes one's own
troubled heart. Yet the economy of language is stag-
gering. No metaphors extended, or images tracked to
their lair; no syllables wasted, no digressions, no ex-
planations. Does this mean the book lies close to the
origins of writing? To a time of scant or intractable
resources? Think of vellum—how the bookmaker
required the hides of two hundred sheep to make a
single illuminated gospel in early Christian Ireland.
Think of inscriptions cut painstakingly into stone,
bamboo stalk, or fragile tortoiseshell. In ancient
India, craftsmen devised books of pressed palmyra or

plantain leaves. These they incised with a metal stylus, washed with ink made of lampblack and vegetable oil, then bound with a cord strung through one or two holes drilled in the stack of brittle leaves. Two wooden boards, sandwiching the pages, formed the covers, which were painted and sometimes incised with exacting motifs.

At the time the *Amarushataka* was compiled, writing systems had been present in India for hundreds of years. South Asia's hot, humid climate, with its torrential monsoon rains, profligate molds and bacteria, and omnivorous insects, has been ruinous for old manuscripts, however, making it difficult to know how prevalent writing was in the eighth century. But at a court where poetry stood in high regard, where a prince or warlord like Amaru himself took an active interest in writing poetry, there would surely have been scribes employed in the production of books.

The poems of the *Amarushataka* may have circulated in written form from the time of their composition, perhaps accompanied by collaborative illustrations from artists or painters. Several handmade manuscripts of the anthology include colorful miniature paintings. I saw one such manuscript on display in the archaeological museum of Bhubaneswar in 1993. Rather than using Devanagari, the more common script for Sanskrit, a scribe had reproduced it in the Oriyan alphabet, the script used throughout Orissa State. The Chhatrapati Shivaji Maharaj Vastu

Sangrahalaya museum in Mumbai (formerly the Prince of Wales Museum of Western India) also houses an illustrated edition. Judging by a published description of the manuscript, as well as by reproductions of a few of its miniature paintings that I've had the good fortune to see, the copy is a cultural treasure. Its paintings have flat, bold fields of color; its drama is restrained and dignified.

Yet we don't really know how these terse poems appeared to their first audience. Like Native American song or Japanese haiku—other poetic traditions known for their crystalline and compressed verses—the original impulse of Sanskrit verse probably lay in oral performance. Poems, including those of the *Amarushataka*, could have been sung or formally chanted, with phrases and lines repeated, with musical embellishment or the insertion of nonsensical vocables. Intriguingly, one manuscript of the *Amarushataka* housed in the British Library has been bound together with a treatise on music.

Sanskrit drama of the period—in formal ways close to the Buddhist-inspired Noh plays of Japan—might provide a clue. In Sanskrit theater, action and dialogue come to a pregnant halt several times during each act, at moments of intense emotional pitch. An actor then slowly intones a four-line verse to musical accompaniment and performs a dance of concentrated grace and intensity. Since the earliest treatises on India's aesthetics address theater specifically, some scholars see this as the origin of Indian poetry. The multifaceted, primordial art of the theater or the ritual dance slowly divided, and the separate arts, poetry one of them, went off to develop on their own.

As far as I've been able to discover, the *Amarushataka* as a whole has not been translated into English-language poetry before this edition. A few prose versions with no pretense to poetry appeared in India last century. Why has it not been translated in England or the United States? Given its status in India as one of the classic collections of verse, I see its nonappearance in the West as part of a long-standing neglect, even dismissal, of South Asia by official American and European culture.

India has made exceptional contributions to music, art, poetry, religion, cooking, medicine, mathematics, linguistics, and philosophy for at least four millennia. Yet the South Asian Studies departments in our universities subsist on starvation budgets. The languages go little acknowledged; the geography remains terra incognita to most outsiders. Fortunately, a dedicated counterculture or nonofficial effort keeps India, her arts, and her religious traditions visible in the West, especially since the 1960s. With Ravi Shankar's U.S. tour in 1965, then his notable friendship with George Harrison, India's music became widely known and readily available. In its wake, a steady interest in India's poetry has endured. I hope this little book can contribute to that nonofficial effort to make known the achievements of South Asia's arts.

As a poet, not a South Asia expert, I have worked at the Sanskrit language for twenty-odd years. I had encountered some of Amaru's poems in other anthologies—even translated a few of them—but not until I began to work with the full collection did I detect how carefully articulated the book is. If these poems intrigue you, you can find further accounts of the *Amarushataka* and Sanskrit poetry in general by looking through my bibliography. I've noted some of the books that proved useful in recent years, as well as those translations that strike me as commendable poetry.

In their original Sanskrit, each of the *Amarushataka* poems is a four-line verse. They occur in complex metrical patterns, with a distinct preference for the one known as *shardula-vikridita*, "tiger's play." About two thirds of the poems are set in this meter, which has nineteen syllables to a line. It would be crazy to try to reproduce in English translation either the cadence or the intricate sound combinations of the far-away tongue.

The Sanskrit sounds like this:

dampatyor niśi jalpator gṛhaśukenākarṇitaṃ
  yad vacas

tat prātar gurusaṁnidhau nigadatas
   tasyātimātram vadhūḥ
karṇālambitapadmaragaśakalaṁ
   vinyasya cañcūpuṭe
vrīḍārtā vidadhāti dāḍimaphalavyājena
   vāgbandhanam

(v. 15)

I hold to John Dryden's wry observation in his essay "On Translation": "A good poet is no more like himself in dull translation than his carcass would be to a living body." Accordingly, I want to breathe the thirteen-hundred-year-old lyrics into life as contemporary poems. The crankiest translator wouldn't try to wrench some modern language into tiger's play— an act that that could only tempt the displeasure of the gods.

Four versions of the *Amarushataka* exist. They contain different numbers of verses, from 96 to 115. In many respects it is a leaky book. Some of its notable poems show up attributed to other poets in anthologies compiled centuries after the *Amarushataka*. Some of them occur with confounding changes in vocabulary or meter, enough that one wonders if the two versions are not separate poems. Surviving manuscripts come with mistakes or omissions, the result of sloppy transcription.

I have handled and compared several editions in the British Oriental and India Office, housed in the

British Library in London; in the end I decided to work exclusively with the southern Indian version. This was edited with a commentary by Vemabhupala sometime between 1403 and 1420, and published in a modern, critically edited edition in 1959 by C. R. Devadhar (who also provides a nearly impenetrable English prose retelling of each verse). The number of poems in Vemabhupala's version, one hundred and one, feels satisfying—like the expression "forever and a day."

Scholars now believe that Vemabhupala, working nearly seven centuries after Amaru, had a somewhat larger manuscript at his disposal than those that have come down to our own times. He discarded at least fifteen poems, possibly more, considering them spurious or not up to Amaru's standard. Vemabhupala writes that he established his version after "having gathered the root poems and tossed out [later] insertions" (*mulaślokam samāhṛtya prakśiptān parihṛtya ca*). His acid test was, I suppose, his singular instinct for poetry.

In addition, Vemabhupala rearranged the order of the poems. His sequence ends up substantially different from the other three versions. He also composed a commentary, the *Shringara-dipika* or "Lamp of Eros," in which he sedulously discusses elements of each verse. A good and restrained annotator, he intended his "lamp" to light up, not interpret the poems. Its purpose was simply to help a reader through baffling turns of grammar or odd vocabulary, to highlight subtleties and suggestions in the poems, and provide the names of their meters.

In Vemabhupala's edition, the four opening verses conjure the principal gods of classical India. This is a convention in Sanskrit works of scholarship, religion, science, or literature. But to open the *Amarushataka* with these particular verses introduces a touch of humor—humor or something slyer? Did Amaru—or Vemabhupala—mean them to be playful? Subversive? Philosophical? Anticlerical? If you look back at verses three and four, pause for a moment over them. From the charged encounter of human sexual partners, the powerful pantheon of Hindu gods gets dismissed—abruptly, forcefully, unsentimentally—their powers declared irrelevant. This could be a moment from the *Upanishads*, when the esoteric teachings stand revealed: the old gods, potent as they seem in religion or myth, have no dominion over the surge of instincts that govern our actual lives. Confronted by something so starkly elemental, the gods of conventional religion are exposed as irrelevant.

In the *Amarushataka,* this archaic force seems at first glance to be basic human sexual affection, with an emphasis on the wounds that drive men and women to frenzy. But could it be a more-than-human passion the poems conjure? Do we stand in the domain known as ecstasy of love, *kamananda?* Or have we entered what yogins call *paramananda,* the ecstasy beyond love, to which sexual love is but the gateway?

Here I feel we have come to the edge of a great mystery, and the poems of the *Amarushataka* disappear like tracks into a confounding wilderness. This must be the point that one of the poems arrives at when its poet, confronting his lover's desperate mix of desire and torment, declares: "What she then did, no poet's words command the power to tell."

BIBLIOGRAPHY

Works in Sanskrit

Amaruśatakam. With the Sanskrit commentary "Rasikasañjīvinī" by Arjunavarmadeva. Edited by Narayana Rama Acharya "Kavyatirtha." Mumbai: Nirnaya Sagara Press, 1954.

Amaruśatakam. With the Sanskrit commentary "Sṛṅgāradīpikā" of Vemabhūpāla. Critically edited with an introduction, English translation, and appendices by Chintaman Ramchandra Devadhar. 1959. Reprint, New Delhi: Motilal Banarsidass, 1984.

Amaruśatakam. British Library, Or. 3566. Palm leaf ms. in straight-topped Nepalese writing, 15th–16th century.

Amaruśatakam. British Library, IO SAN 1503d. Manuscript of Arjunavarmadeva's edition, bound with two other texts, no date.

Kavikaṇṭhābharaṇa by *Kṣemendra*. Edited by Vāmana Keśava Lele, M.A. New Delhi: Motilal Banarsidass, 1967. This twelfth-century text by the

renowned poet Kśemendra served as a handbook
of instruction for poets. It includes guidelines for
composition and for study, a discussion of appro-
priate themes, and detailed recommendations for
how a poet should utilize the hours of the day, with
adequate time set aside for writing, contempla-
tion, and lovemaking.

The Subhāṣitaratnakoṣa. Compiled by Vidyākara.
Edited by D. D. Kosambi and V. V. Gokhale. Cam-
bridge: Harvard University Press, 1957. One of the
finest compilations of classical Sanskrit poetry. Its
1,738 verses were collected by Vidyākara, abbot of
a Buddhist monastery in Bengal, in the eleventh
century.

MONIER-WILLIAMS, SIR MONIER. *A Sanskrit-
English Dictionary.* Oxford: Oxford University
Press, 1899.

Works in English

CHANDRA, DR. MOTI. "An Illustrated Set of the
Amaru-śataka." *Bulletin of the Prince of Wales Mu-
seum of Western India*, no. 2 (1953): 1–63.

DAUMAL, RENÉ. *RASA, or Knowledge of the Self:
Essays on Indian Aesthetics and Selected Sanskrit
Studies.* Translated with an introduction by Louise
Landes Levi. New York: New Directions, 1982. An

inspiring and cranky book by the only poet of the European avant-garde to seriously study Sanskrit. Daumal found in yoga and Sanskrit poetics a way out of the perilous drug experiments of his youth, and a method for writing poetry.

HEIFETZ, HANK. *The Origin of the Young God: Kālidāsa's Kumārasaṃbhava.* Berkeley: University of California Press, 1985. Fine translation. This is Kalidasa's unfinished, long erotic poem on the marriage of Shiva and Parvati. It tells the story of Kama becoming bodiless, and links the earth's geomorphic and biological forces to erotic love.

INGALLS, DANIEL H. H. *Sanskrit Poetry from Vidyākara's "Treasury."* Cambridge: Harvard University Press, 1968. Ingalls' introduction remains one of the best accounts of Sanskrit poetry as a whole. Good translations. This is a paperback selection from his complete *An Anthology of Sanskrit Court Poetry*, published in 1965, also from Harvard.

INGALLS, DANIEL H. H., JEFFREY MASSON, AND M. V. PATWARDHAN, trans. *The* Dhvanyāloka *of* Ānandavardhana with the Locana *of Abhinava-gupta.* Edited with an introduction by Daniel H. H. Ingalls. Cambridge: Harvard University Press, 1990. Two philosophical-critical texts by the principal figures of Kashmiri Shaivism, with many examples of poetry ably translated. Includes the first mention of the poet Amaru.

LIENHARD, SIEGFRIED. *A History of Classical Poetry Sanskrit-Pali-Prakrit.* Wiesbaden, Germany: Otto Harrassowitz, 1984. The most thorough scholarly study of classical Indian poetry. Good for its clarification of terms and discussion of principal works.

MASSON, J. MOUSAIEFF and W. S. MERWIN. *The Peacock's Egg: Love Poems from Ancient India.* San Francisco: North Point Press, 1981. Out of print, but a delightful selection of poems with a spirited cross-cultural introduction by Jeff Masson. The authors have selected greatest-hits poems, but also drawn surprising examples from out-of-the-way sources.

MILLER, BARBARA STOLLER. *Bhartrihari: Poems.* New York: Columbia University Press, 1967. Bhartrihari wrote three *shatakas,* collections of one hundred poems, on three topics: worldly counsel, love, and renunciation. He was one of the vivid and troubled personalities in Sanskrit poetry. Miller's translations are fresh and scrupulous. Miller was one of the luminaries of Sanskrit scholarship—her translations are indispensable. See her renditions of Jayadeva, Kalidasa, and Bilhana as well.

PAZ, OCTAVIO. *In Light of India.* Translated by Eliot Weinberger. Orlando, Fla.: Harcourt Brace, 1995.

Paz served as Mexico's ambassador to India and has written widely on his experiences and studies there. See his chapter "The Hermit and the Lover" for the Nobel Prize–winning poet's insightful encounter with the motivating forces of Sanskrit poetry. Includes ten poems translated.

SCHELLING, ANDREW. *The Cane Groves of Narmada River: Erotic Poems from Old India.* San Francisco: City Lights, 1998. One hundred poems translated from the Sanskrit and related vernacular traditions. The introduction argues that in India there has existed an intimate, though infrequently examined, relationship between erotic poetry and ecological literacy.

————. *Wild Form, Savage Grammar: Poetry, Ecology, Asia.* Albuquerque, N.Mex.: La Alameda Press, 2003. A collection of essays that includes several on Sanskrit poetry and other Asian traditions. Places a watchful eye on the connection of verse traditions to current topics in ecology and nature writing, and on Asiatic influences on art and philosophy in North America.

SELBY, MARTHA ANN. *Grow Long Blessed Night: Love Poems from Classical India.* Oxford: Oxford University Press, 2000. Poems from the *Amarushataka* compared with lyrics from two earlier Indian traditions—classical Tamil and the Prakrit

Gaha-kosa. Selby's essays are scholarly and enthusiastic, her translations brisk and contemporary.

SHANKAR, RAVI. *Raga Mala: An Autobiography*. Edited and introduced by George Harrison. New York: Welcome Rain Publishers, 1999. Endearing account of his own life by the musician who has done more than anyone else to bring a sense of India's artistic heritage to the West. Shankar provides a practicing artist's look at the rigorous training required for competency in India's traditional arts.

Andrew Schelling is the author of fifteen books and chapbooks, the most recent a collection of essays, *Wild Form, Savage Grammar*, which explores the karmic connection between Asia's poetic traditions and North American culture. Living in the foothills of Colorado's Front Range, he studies at the feet of the glacially carved Indian Peaks and is active on ecology issues in the Southern Rockies. He received a B.A. in 1975 from the University of California, Santa Cruz, then pursued Sanskrit at Berkeley, later traveling through India and the Himalayas, as well as to libraries in Europe and America to do research. His translations of India's classical poetry appear in numerous anthologies. The Academy of American Poets gave him their Harold Morton Landon Translation Award for *Dropping the Bow: Poems from Ancient India* in 1992. He has received two translation grants from the Witter Bynner Foundation for Poetry, and his own poetry has been rendered into French, German, Spanish, and Dutch. Since 1990 he has taught at Naropa University's Jack Kerouac School in Boulder.

Also by

ANDREW SCHELLING